Defending Faith

⌘

Lenten Devotions

Edited and compiled

by Dr. Jeffrey P. Johnson

DEFENDING FAITH LENTEN DEVOTIONS
Edited and compiled by Dr. Jeffrey P. Johnson

Cover design by Erin Newton

ISBN 987-0-89367-297-3

© 2009
For Men's Ministries International
By Light and Life Communications
Indianapolis, Indiana
Printed in the U.S.A.

DEDICATION

To my dear friends, Oklahoma State Senator Mike and Noel Mazzei and my adorable godchildren, Maria, Carissa, Caleb, Mykaela and Jackson.

May they grow in grace and guard the good deposit that is in them.

You then, my son, be strong in the grace that is in Christ Jesus. And the things you have heard me say in the presence of many witnesses entrust to reliable men who will also be qualified to teach others.

2 Timothy 2:1-2

The Gentiles praise Thee that Thy Word has become a mirror before them, that in it they might see death, secretly swallowing up their lives. But graven images were being adorned by their artificers; and by their adornments were disfiguring their adorners. But Thou didst draw them to Thy cross; and while the beauties of the body were disfigured upon it, the beauties of the mind shone forth upon it. Then, as for the Gentiles who used to go after gods which were no gods, He Who was by a bridle, turned them from many gods to the One. This is that Mighty One, Whose preaching became a bridle in the jaws of the Gentiles, and led them away from idols to Him that sent Him.

Ephraem Syrus
c.306-373

INTRODUCTION

Jesus Christ commanded the apostles to go into "the world and make disciples." He said this after spending three and a half years with them in a variety of situations and experiences. He challenged their thinking and their way of living. He taught them how to walk by faith, trust in the grace of God and love the people around them. He encouraged them, rebuked them, empowered them and served them. They learned what it meant to be a disciple of Jesus Christ and passed on this faith to the next generation of believers. As the Apostle Paul said to Timothy: *"What you heard from me, keep as the pattern of sound teaching, with faith and love in Christ Jesus. Guard the good deposit that was entrusted to you — guard it with the help of the Holy Spirit who lives in us"* (2 Timothy 1:13-14).

Receive the faith. Live the faith. Share the faith. Guard the faith. The purpose of this book is to introduce the reader to those faithful disciples of the fourth and fifth century who defended the faith from forces inside and outside the church. In the book *Emerging Faith Lenten Devotions*[1] the reader was exposed to the Apostolic and Church Fathers from 96 A.D. to 300 A.D., including Clement of Rome, Ignatius, Irenaeus, Origen, Tertullian and Cyprian. In this book, *Defending Faith Lenten Devotions*, the reader can explore the church leaders from 301 A.D. to 460 A.D., including Eusebius, Athanasius, Augustine, Chrysostom and Jerome. The church at this time was struggling with persecution (political and religious), rapid expansion, christological heresies and fashionable faith living. These fourth- and fifth-century disciples helped to formulate the New Testament; debated creeds and doctrines; created liturgy and worship styles; promoted virginity, chastity and holiness; and developed faith communities in metropolitan areas as well as desert mountains.[2] They guarded the faith from the likes of Gnosticism (secret truths),

Docetism (Christ's human body), Arianism (Christ inferior to God), Apollinarianism (Christ's human nature), Montanism (excessive spiritual gifting), Pelagianism (human nature), Manichaeanism (a form of Gnosticism) and Donatism (holiness in the church).[3] They often did this from a very practical point of view — these were pastors, lay leaders, secretaries, bishops and historians from Africa, Asia Minor, the Middle East and Europe. They preached, prayed, sang, shared and celebrated their faith, and when there were collisions between their faith and culture, or their faith in its context, they rose up and guarded the good deposit.[4] Like church leaders from other times and places, they faced temptations from pride, abuse of authority, competition, lack of discipline, biblical ignorance and sexual misconduct.[5]

The beginning of the fourth century saw the most intense persecution the church had ever seen by the Roman Empire. It centered on Caesar worship and the decision to pledge your loyalty to the emperor of Rome or to Jesus of Nazareth. Many disciples were arrested, maimed and killed because they declared "Jesus is Lord." Yet the fourth century also saw the Edict of Milan, which ended formal Roman persecution, and the beginning of a state-sponsored church. Eusebius, the great church historian, experienced these events firsthand and forever recorded the testimony of the faithful ones who overcame by the blood of the Lamb and the word of faith.

The remainder of the fourth century and the fifth century also saw the rise of religious persecution like never before. People like Athanasius, Cyril and John Chrysostom were victims of violent and even deadly church politics. They set apart Christ as Lord in their hearts (1 Peter 3:15) and faced down heretics, despots, tyrants and apostates. They suffered for doing good under the hands of other Christians. John Chrysostom was dragged from his pulpit during a baptismal service on Easter eve because he refused to condone the injustices done by the government. He died a martyr.

The 160 years covered in this devotional book is not a very long time, and many of the leaders of the fourth and fifth centuries knew each other and developed relationships with each other. Eusebius' relationship with the Emperor Constantine kept him out of trouble during the Arian debate. Augustine wrote to Jerome and even exhorted him to be more gracious on the issues of sex and marriage. Gregory of Nazianzus met Basil in school and became lifelong friends. Gregory of Nyssa visited Cyril in Jerusalem and found his doctrine true and sound. Of course, Ambrose pastored Augustine and led him to Christ after he went through a crisis event. One of the most celebrated relationships of the fourth century is between Athanasius and Antony. When Athanasius was exiled from Alexandria and faced persecution from the Arians, it was Antony who left his desert hermitage to go and encourage his friend.[6]

The influence of female leadership in the fourth and fifth centuries is hidden but very powerful and very godly. Leaders like Helena, Constantine's mother, who refused to follow Roman customs of political marriages and became a single mom full of grace. She influenced her son through prayer and devotion, and helped to build churches all over the Roman Empire. Monica, Augustine's mother, followed her son all over that empire interceding for his salvation. Her prayers were answered when her son became a Christian before she died. Both of these godly women impacted the world through their sons. Jerome writes a testimony of Paula who served the Lord in Palestine and took up her cross to follow Christ. Anthusa, John Chrysostom's mother, raised her two children in the faith after her husband died. Macrina, Gregory and Basil's sister, dialogues her faith in the book *On the Soul and the Resurrection* and was honored for her charity and good works. She was named for her grandmother, who helped her daughter (Emmelia) raise 10 children after their father died. Two of those children became bishops of the church.

An attempt has been made to avoid the "hagiographic ideal" in devotional reading.[7] Hagiography is a style of writing from the early church, which highlights deeds and character that encourage other disciples to grow closer to God. Signs, wonders and miracles are often recited to show the power of God at work in everyday people. Several examples of the supernatural power of God are included in this devotional book like Constantine's vision or Gregory of Nyssa's dream. This book also contains same of the friction found in church and ministry including Augustine and Pelagius; John Chrysostom and the Empress; and even Eusebius and Athanasius. These men and women were faithful servants of God but had their weaknesses, troubles and even foibles as well. In the end they (like all Christians) relied completely on the grace of Christ Jesus.

The impact of these saints defending the faith can still be felt today. They helped define sound doctrine (Nicene Creed), original sin (Augustine), free will (Pelagius) and the nature of Christ (Athanasius). They developed liturgy for worship (Chrysostom/Basil), teachings for baptism (Cyril), autobiographies (Augustine), hagiographies (Athanasius on Antony) and church histories (Eusebius and others). They standardized the New Testament and produced a version that lasted more than 1,000 years (Jerome). They held conferences and councils on controversial issues and pro-duced a faith that continued to seek God for understanding and was worthy of sharing with others. Some of them were reluctant, others were rascals, but they guarded the good deposit in them.

The Holy Spirit helps each generation of disciples to guard the good deposit. This book is a witness to their sacrifice, obedience and love as they lived together and defended the faith.[8]

APOSTOLIC FATHERS

Clement of Rome – c. 96 A.D.

A Letter to Diognetus from a Disciple – c. 110 A.D.

Polycarp – c. 69-155

The Martyrdom of Polycarp – c. 155 A.D.

Ignatius of Antioch – c. 107

Barnabas of Alexandria – c. 125 A.D.

Justin Martyr – c. 100-165

Irenaeus – c. 130-200

Hermas – c. 160

Tatian of Rome – c. 160

Theophilus of Antioch – c. 168

Athenagoras – c. 177

Clement of Alexandria – c. 150-215

Tertullian – c. 160-225

Perpetua – d. 203

Minucius Felix – c. 250-311

Commodianus – d. 240

Origen – c. 185-254

Novatian of Rome – c. 250

Origen – c. 185-254

Hippolytus – c. 170-236

Cyprian – d. 258

Dionysuis the Great – d. 264

Methodius of Olympus – d. 311

Gregory Thaumaturgus – c. 205-265

Peter, Bishop of Alexandria – c. 260-311

These Apostolic Fathers are chronicled in *Emerging Faith Lenten Devotions,* which examines the first 300 years of the Christian faith.

ASH WEDNESDAY

Character

*"I want to know Christ and the power of his resurrection and
the fellowship of sharing in his sufferings, becoming like him in his
death, and so, somehow, to attain to the resurrection from the
dead."*
Philippians 3:10-11

I come now to the passion itself, which is often cast
in our teeth as a reproach: that we worship a man, and
one who was visited and tormented with remarkable
punishment: that I may show that this very passion was
undergone by Him in accordance with a great and divine
plan, and that goodness and truth and wisdom are
contained in it alone. For if He had been most happy on
the earth, and had reigned through all His life in the
greatest prosperity, no wise man would either have
believed Him to be a God, or judged Him worthy of
divine honour: which is the case with those who are
destitute of true divinity, who not only look up to perish-
able riches, and frail power, and the advantages arising
from the benefit of another, but even consecrate them,
and knowingly do service to the memory of the dead,
worshipping fortune when it is now extinguished, which
the wise never regarded as an object of worship even
when alive and present with them. For nothing among
earthly things can be venerable and worthy of heaven;
but it is virtue alone, and justice alone, which can be
judged a true, and heavenly, and perpetual good, because it is neither given to any one, nor taken away. And
since Christ came upon earth, supplied with virtue and
righteousness, yea rather, since He Himself is virtue, and

Himself righteousness, He descended that He might
teach it and mould the character of man.

Lactantius

c. 260-330

Lactantius was a teacher of rhetoric in Nicomedia before
converting to the Christian faith around 303 A.D. His birth name
was Lucius Caeluis Firmianus Lactantius, and he studied
under Arnolius in North Africa before moving to the coast of
the Adriatic Sea.

THURSDAY AFTER ASH WEDNESDAY

Boundaries

You, my brothers, were called to be free. But do not use your freedom to indulge the sinful nature; rather, serve one another in love. The entire law is summed up in a single command: "Love your neighbor as yourself." If you keep on biting and devouring each other, watch out or you will be destroyed by each other.
Galatians 5:13-15

Fear, love, joy, sadness, lust, eager desire, anger, pity, emulation, admiration — these motions or affections of the mind exist from the beginning of man's creation by the Lord; and they were usefully and advantageously introduced into human nature, that by governing himself by these with method, and in accordance with reason, man may be able, by acting manfully, to exercise those good qualities, by means of which he would justly have deserved to receive from the Lord eternal life. For these affections of the mind being restrained within their proper limits, that is, being rightly employed, produce at present good qualities, and in the future eternal rewards. But when they advance beyond their boundaries, that is, when they turn aside to an evil course, then vices and iniquities come forth, and produce everlasting punishments.

Lactantius
c. 260-330

Lactantius was called upon to educate Crispus, Emperor Constantine's son, around 315 A.D. During this time he wrote several works including *The Christian Institutes* in which he dwells on the righteousness of Jesus Christ, true worship, judgment and eternal life. He also wrote a treatise on the workmanship of God as an attempt to prove God's goodness and wisdom from God's creation of the human body and soul.

FRIDAY AFTER ASH WEDNESDAY

Following Christ

Then he called the crowd to him along with his disciples and said: "If anyone would come after me, he must deny himself and take up his cross and follow me. For whoever wants to save his life will lose it, but whoever loses his life for me and for the gospel will save it. What good is it for man to gain the whole world, yet forfeit his soul? Or what can a man give in exchange for his soul?"
Mark 8:34-37

Every one therefore who learns any art, when he sees his master by his diligence and skill perfecting his art, does himself earnestly endeavour to make what he takes in hand like to it. If he is not able, he is not perfected in his work. We therefore who have a Master, our Lord Jesus Christ, why do we not follow His doctrine? — since He renounced repose, pleasure, glory, riches, pride, the power of revenge, His mother and brethren, nay, and moreover His own life, on account of His piety towards His Father, and His love to us the race of mankind; and suffered not only persecution and stripes, reproach and mockery, but also crucifixion, that He might save the penitent, both Jews and Gentiles. If therefore He for our sakes renounced His repose, was not ashamed of the cross, and did not esteem death inglorious, why do not we imitate His sufferings, and renounce on His account even our own life, with that patience which He gives us?
Apostolic Constitutions
c. 340

The *Apostolic Constitutions* is a collection of church law and ordinances from Syria ranging from the third and fourth centuries. It is divided into eight books with the first six books being the oldest and the last books being written around 340 A.D. The topics include morals, discipline, worship and the order of service for baptism and communion. The *Apostolic Constitutions* reflects on early church leadership and connects Jewish customs with Christian practices.

SATURDAY AFTER ASH WEDNESDAY

Vice and Virtue

"I tell you the truth, unless a kernel of wheat falls to the ground and dies, it remains only a single seed. But if it dies, it produces many seeds. The man who loves his life will lose it, while the man who hates his life in this world will keep it for eternal life. Whoever serves me must follow me; and where I am, my servant also will be. My Father will honor the one who serves me."
John 12:24-26

Ye see therefore, my children, how that there are two in all things, one against the other, and the one is hidden by the other. Death succeedeth to life, dishonour to glory, night to day, and darkness to light; and all things are under the day, and just things under life: wherefore also everlasting life awaiteth death. Nor may it be said that truth is a lie, nor right wrong; for all truth is under the light, even as all things are under God. All these things I proved in my life, and I wandered not from the truth of the Lord, and I searched out the commandments of the Most High, walking with singleness of face according to all my strength unto that which is good.

Testament of the 12 Patriarchs
c. 300

This work is modeled on Jacob's testament and blessing found in Genesis 49 and deals with morality, holiness and faith. Some scholars believe it was written as early as 200 B.C. in Hebrew and Aramiac, and was translated into Greek by Christians around 150 A.D. It is quoted by Tertullian and Origen and was held with considerable respect by the early church. This passage comes from *The Testament of Asher Concerning the Two Faces of Vice and Virtue* and encourages the reader to be of single heart and single mind.

OLD TESTAMENT APOCRYPHA

Tobit
Judith
The Additions to the Book of Esther
Wisdom of Solomon
Ecclesiasticus, or the Wisdom of Jesus Son of Sirach
Baruch
The Letter of Jeremiah
The Additions to the Book of Daniel
The Prayer of Azariah and the Song of the Three Jews
Susanna
Bel and the Dragon
   1 Maccabees
   2 Maccabees
1 Esdras
Prayer of Manasseh
Psalm 151
3 Maccabees
2 Esdras
4 Maccabees

FIRST SUNDAY OF LENT

Apocrypha of the New Testament

"Dear friends, do not believe every spirit, but test the spirits to see whether they are from God, because many false prophets have gone out into the world. This is how you can recognize the Spirit of God: Every spirit that acknowledges that Jesus Christ has come in the flesh is from God, but every spirit that does not acknowledge Jesus is not from God. This is the spirit of the antichrist, which you have heard is coming and even now is already in the world."
1 John 4:1-3

The following are a list of early Christian books that are not considered a part of the New Testament. Many of these titles were written around 200-300 A.D. and focus on the history of Joseph and Mary; the infancy of Jesus Christ; the history of Pilate; or letters on doctrine and faith including the end times. Many of these writings still exist, and some have found popularity in the latter half of the 20th century.

Apocryphal Gospels
1. The Gospel of Pseudo-Matthew
2. The Gospel of the Nativity of Mary
3. The History of Joseph the Carpenter
4. The Gospel of Thomas
5. The Arabic Gospel of the Infancy of the Savior
6. The Gospel of Nicodemus
7. The Letter of Pontius Pilate
8. The Report of Pontius the Procurator
9. The Report of Pontius Pilate
10. The Giving Up on Pontius Pilate
11. The Death of Pilate
12. The Narrative of Joseph
13. The Avenging of the Savior

MONDAY, FIRST WEEK OF LENT

Apocrypha of the New Testament

This is the disciple who testifies to these things and who wrote them down. We know that his testimony is true. Jesus did many other things as well. If every one of them were written down, I suppose that even the whole world would not have room for the books that would be written.
John 21:24-25

The word apocrypha means "hidden" or "secret," and this is used to describe both New Testament and Old Testament writings that did not make the final cut into the Holy Scriptures. The New Testament came into existence between 47 A.D. and 250 A.D. with 27 books in the final edition. The standard for Holy Scripture included spiritual content, doctrinal soundness, divine inspiration, usage (by early church Christians) and apostolic connections (was it written by an apostle?). Many of the Apocryphal New Testament books were associated with gnostic Christianity and thus barred from the Bible.

Other New Testament Apocryphal Works
1. Acts of the Holy Apostles Peter and Paul
2. Acts of Paul and Thecla
3. Acts of Barnabas
4. Acts of Philip
5. Acts of Andrew
6. Acts of Andrew and Matthias
7. Acts of Peter and Andrew
8. Acts of St. Matthew
9. Acts of Thomas
10. Acts of Bartholomew
11. Acts of Thaddeus

12. Acts of John
13. Revelation of Moses
14. Revelation of Esdras
15. Revelation of Paul
16. Revelation of John
17. The Passing of Mary

TUESDAY, FIRST WEEK OF LENT

Church History

"You are the salt of the earth. But if the salt loses its saltiness, how can it be made salty again? It is no longer good for anything, except to be thrown out and trampled by men."
Matthew 5:13

It is my purpose to write an account of the successions of the holy apostles, as well as of the times which have elapsed from the days of our Saviour to our own; and to relate the many important events which are said to have occurred in the history of the Church; and to mention those who have governed and presided over the Church in the most prominent parishes, and those who in each generation have proclaimed the divine word either orally or in writing. It is my purpose also to give the names and number and times of those who through love of innovation have run into the greatest errors, and, proclaiming themselves discoverers of knowledge falsely so-called have like fierce wolves unmercifully devastated the flock of Christ.
Eusebius
d. 380

Eusebius Pamphili of Caesarea is called the "Father of Church History" because of his writings on the early church. He was tutored by Pamphilus who died for the faith around 310 A.D. In Palestine, Eusebius fled the persecution and traveled to Tyre and then Egypt, where he was arrested and imprisoned for being a follower of Jesus Christ. This was great persecution by Diocletian, which affected the entire Roman Empire. During this terrible period of history Christians were not only killed for their faith, but many were tortured and left maimed and mutilated.

What he witnessed and experienced he also wrote down, so

that the world would remember how the disciples suffered for doing good. They returned love for evil and blessed the church for generations to come by their courage and patient endurance.

WEDNESDAY, FIRST WEEK OF LENT

Martyrs

*"You are the light of the world. A city on a hill cannot be
hidden. Neither do people light a lamp and put it under a bowl.
Instead they put it on its stand, and it gives light to everyone in the
house. In the same way, let your light shine before men, that they
may see your good deeds and praise your Father in heaven."*
Matthew 5:14-16

Why need we mention the rest by name, or number the
multitude of the men, or picture the various sufferings of the
admirable martyrs of Christ? Some of them were slain with
the axe, as in Arabia. The limbs of some were broken, as in
Cappadocia. Some, raised on high by the feet, with their
heads down, while a gentle fire burned beneath them, were
suffocated by the smoke which arose from the burning
wood, as was done in Mesopotamia. Others were mutilated
by cutting off their noses and ears and hands, and cutting to
pieces the other members and parts of their bodies, as in
Alexandria.

Eusebius

d. 380

After Eusebius was released from prison he returned to
Caesarea and became bishop around 313 A.D. Local persecution
continued in this part of the Roman Empire (around Palestine)
until 323 A.D. when the Emperor Constantine defeated the
Emperor Licinius.

The Arian controversy was evolving in this part of the world as
well. Around 318 A.D., the debate over the nature of Christ
gained momentum in Egypt and soon spread to the whole
Eastern church (Syria and Asia Minor). Arius was excommuni-
cated by the Bishop of Alexandria, but dialogue and debate

continued for several decades with Eusebius initially support-
ing Arius against the Egyptians. Eventually, he accepted the
Nicene Creed in 325 A.D., which challenged the tenets of
Arianism. He was strongly encouraged to do so by his friend
Emperor Constantine.

FRIDAY, FIRST WEEK OF LENT

Constantine

For rulers hold no terror for those who do right, but for those who do wrong. Do you want to be free from fear of the one in authority? Then do what is right and he will commend you. For he is God's servant to do you good. But if you do wrong, be afraid, for he does not bear the sword for nothing. He is God's servant, an agent of wrath to bring punishment on the wrongdoer. Therefore, it is necessary to submit to the authorities, not only because of possible punishment but also because of conscience. This is also why you pay taxes, for the authorities are God's servants, who give their full time to governing. Give everyone what you owe him: If you owe taxes, pay taxes; if revenue, then revenue; if respect, then respect; if honor, then honor. Let no debt remain outstanding, except the continuing debt to love one another, for he who loves his fellowman has fulfilled the law.
Romans 13:3-8

He then lifted his voice and poured forth a strain of thanksgiving to God; after which he added these words. "Now I know that I am truly blessed: now I feel assured that I am accounted worthy of immortality, and am made a partaker of Divine light." He further expressed his compassion for the unhappy condition of those who were strangers to such blessings as he enjoyed. ...
Eusebius
d. 380

Eusebius was a faithful follower of Jesus Christ and a great supporter of Emperor Constantine. Eusebius was condemned for supporting Arianism during a meeting in Antioch but was reinstated by Constantine himself after producing a baptismal creed as evidence of his sound doctrine. The emperor called on

Eusebius several times for wisdom and advice, and even sent him to Jerusalem to dedicate the Church of the Resurrection.

The reading above is from the death of Constantine who reserved his baptism until he was on his deathbed (often called a deferment of baptism). After being baptized, Constantine refused to wear his royal robes and died at noon on the day of Pentecost, 337 A.D.

SATURDAY, FIRST WEEK OF LENT

First Draft

You must teach what is in accord with sound doctrine. Teach the older men to be temperate, worthy of respect, self-controlled, and sound in faith, in love and in endurance. Likewise, teach the older women to be reverent in the way they live, not to be slanderers or addicted to much wine, but to teach what is good.
Titus 2:1-3

The Nicene Creed

We believe in one God, the Father Almighty, Maker of all things, visible and invisible:

And in one Lord Jesus Christ, the Son of God, begotten of the Father, only begotten, that is, of the substance of the Father;

God of God; Light of Light; very God of very God; begotten, not made; being of one substance with the Father,

By whom all things were made, both things in heaven and things in earth:

Who for us men and for our salvation came down, and was incarnate, and was made man:

He suffered and rose again the third day:

And ascended into heaven:

And shall come to judge the quick and the dead.

And in the Holy Ghost.

The First Council of Nicaea was convened in 325 A.D. by Emperor Constantine to deal with Arianism. It started in May and lasted more than two months. It was at this council that Arius was condemned, Eusebius was reinstated, Constantine was in charge and the first draft of the Nicene Creed was accepted. It was approved by all the bishops (around 240) except Theonoas of Marmarica and Secundus of Ptolemais.

The Creed was drawn up to defend the faith against Arianism. Arius from Egypt challenged the human nature of Christ, and thus the Nicene Creed has four points that support the nature of Christ and humanity. The Nicene Creed, as most churches have now, was finalized in the fifth century. It is one of the only creeds the major branches of Christianity all agree on (Eastern Orthodox, Roman Catholic and Protestant) and is used every week in churches around the world.

The Nicene Creed (Final Draft)

We believe in one God the Father Almighty,
Maker of heaven and earth, and of all things visible and invisible:

And in one Lord Jesus Christ, the only-begotten Son of God, begotten of His Father before all worlds, God of God, Light of Light, very God of very God, begotten, not made, being of one substance with the Father, by whom all things were made; who for us men and for our salvation came down from heaven, and was incarnate by the Holy Spirit of the Virgin Mary, and was made man, and crucified also for us under Pontius Pilate; He suffered and was buried, and the third day He rose again according to the Scriptures, and ascended into heaven, and sitteth on the right hand of the Father; and He shall come again with glory to judge both the quick and the dead; whose kingdom shall have no end.

And we believe in the Holy Spirit, the Lord and Giver of life, who proceedeth from the Father and the Son, who with the Father and the Son together is worshiped and glorified; who spoke by the prophets. And we believe in one holy catholic and apostolic church; we acknowledge one baptism for the remission of sins, and we look for the resurrection of the dead, and the life of the world to come. Amen.

SECOND SUNDAY OF LENT

Signs

How shall we escape if we ignore such a great salvation? This salvation, which was first announced by the Lord, was confirmed to us by those who heard him. God also testified to it by signs, wonders and various miracles, and gifts of the Holy Spirit distributed according to his will.
Hebrews 2:3-4

In fact, about that part of the day when the sun after posing the meridian begins to decline towards the west, he saw a pillar of light in the heavens, in the form of a cross, on which were inscribed these words, "By This Conquer." The appearance of this sign struck the emperor with amazement and scarcely believing his own eyes, he asked those around him if they beheld the same spectacle; and as they unanimously declared that they did, the emperor's mind was strengthened by this divine and marvelous apparition. On the following night in his slumbers he saw Christ who directed him to prepare a standard according to the pattern of that which had been seen; and to use it against his enemies as an assured trophy of victory.
Socrates Scholasticus
380-450

Socrates Scholasticus was a Greek Church historian born in Constantinople who was a lawyer and wrote biographies on the emperors who followed Constantine. It was a continuation of the work Eusebius started and covers the Roman emperors from 305 to 439 a.d. He also wrote several histories on the ecclesiastical councils but always favored events set in his hometown of Constantinople.

This reading comes from the moment when Constantine saw a

vision of the cross in the evening sky in 312 A.D. The next day
he defeated his rival Maxemtius at the battle of Milvian Bridge.
This became known as the Labarum standard in which
Constantine gave glory to God for his victory in battle.

MONDAY, SECOND WEEK OF LENT

Unity

As a prisoner for the Lord, then, I urge you to live a life worthy of the calling you have received. Be completely humble and gentle; be patient, bearing with one another in the Spirit through the bond of peace. There is one body and one Spirit — just as you were called to one hope when you were called — one Lord, one faith, one baptism.
Ephesians 4:1-5

When the business at Nicaea had been transacted as above related, the priests returned home. The emperor rejoiced exceedingly at the restoration of unity of opinion in the Catholic Church, and desirous of expressing in behalf of himself, his children, and the empire, the gratitude towards God which the unanimity of the bishops inspired, he directed that a house of prayer should be erected to God at Jerusalem near the place called Calvary. At the same time his mother Helena repaired to the city for the purpose of offering up prayer, and of visiting the sacred places. Her zeal for Christianity made her anxious to find the wood which had formed the adorable cross.
Salmaninius Hermias Sozomen
d. 410

Sozomen was a church historian born near Gaza in Palestine and educated by monks before moving to Constantinople. He practiced law before writing a church history on the early fourth century. He drew from the works of Socrates Scholasticus and reported on the missionary effects of the church, including the conversion of the Armenians, Saracens and Goths.

This reading records the ending of the Council of Nicaea and the pilgrimage of Helena (c. 255-330 A.D.) to the Holy Land. She was already more than 70 years old when she arrived in Jerusalem and founded churches on the Mount of Olives and in Bethlehem. Several church historians (Ambrose, Rufinus and Sulpicius) report that she discovered the cross of Christ in Jerusalem.

TUESDAY, SECOND WEEK OF LENT

Authority

When he saw Jesus from a distance, he ran and fell on his knees in front of him. He shouted at the top of his voice, "What do you want with me, Jesus, Son of the Most High God? Swear to God that you won't torture me!" For Jesus had said to him, "Come out of this man, you evil spirit!"
Mark 5:6-8

For even a blind man, if he see not the sun, yet if he but take hold of the warmth the sun gives out, knows that there is a sun above the earth. Thus let our opponents also, even if they believe not as yet, being still blind to the truth, yet at least knowing His power by others who believe, not deny the Godhead of Christ and the Resurrection accomplished by Him. For it is plain that if Christ be dead, He could not be expelling demons and spoiling idols; for a dead man the spirits would not have obeyed. But if they be manifestly expelled by the naming of His name, it must be evident that He is not dead; especially as spirits, seeing even what is unseen by men, could tell if Christ were dead and refuse Him any obedience at all. But as it is, what irreligious men believe not, the spirits see — that He is God, — and hence they fly and fall at His feet, saying just what they uttered when He was in the body: "We know Thee Who Thou art, the Holy One of God."
Athanasius
c. 296-373

Athanasius was the bishop of Alexandria where he was born and raised. He was educated in a Christian home and was ordained a deacon before becoming the secretary to the bishop. He attended the Council of Nicaea in the summer of 325 A.D.

and was elected bishop in 328 A.D. Most of his life was spent defending the faith of the church from Arianism. He died in Alexandria on May 3, 373 A.D.

WEDNESDAY, SECOND WEEK OF LENT

Discipline

*Don't let anyone look down on you because you are young,
but set an example for the believers in speech, in life, in love, in
faith and in purity.*
   1 Timothy 4:12

Thus conducting himself, Antony was beloved by all.
He subjected himself in sincerity to the good men whom he
visited, and learned thoroughly where each surpassed him
in zeal and discipline. He observed the graciousness of one;
the unceasing prayer of another; he took knowledge of
another's freedom from anger and another's loving-
kindness; he gave heed to one as he watched, to another as
he studied; one he admired for his endurance, another for
his fasting and sleeping on the ground; the meekness of
one and the long-suffering of another he watched with
care, while he took note of the piety towards Christ and the
mutual love which animated all. Thus filled, he returned to
his own place of discipline, and henceforth would strive to
unite the qualities of each, and was eager to show in
himself the virtues of all. With others of the same age he
had no rivalry; save this only, that he should not be second
to them in higher things. And this he did so as to hurt the
feelings of nobody, but made them rejoice over him. So all
they of that village and the good men in whose intimacy he
was, when they saw that he was a man of this sort, used to
call him God-beloved. And some welcomed him as a son,
others as a brother.
   Athanasius
   c. 296-373

Athanasius left a wealth of written work including a biography on his friend and hermit Antony of Egypt (c.251-356 A.D.). Antony is often called the father of the monastic movement because in 269 A.D. he gave away all his possessions and committed himself to solitude, fasting and prayer. He desired to live a holy life and helped others form communities of faith to separate themselves from the world and seek the presence of God. He spent most of his life in the desert near the foothills of the Red Sea.

THURSDAY, SECOND WEEK OF LENT

Doctrine

*The Spirit clearly says that in later times some will abandon
the faith and follow deceiving spirits and things taught by demons.*
1 Timothy 4:1

Of all other heresies which have departed from the truth
it is acknowledged that they have but devised a madness,
and their irreligiousness has long since become notorious to
all men. For that their authors went out from us, it plainly
follows, as the blessed John has written, that they never
thought nor now think with us. Wherefore, as saith the
Saviour, in that they gather not with us, they scatter with the
devil, and keep an eye on those who slumber, that, by this
second sowing of their own mortal poison, they may have
companions in death. But, whereas one heresy, and that the
last, which has now risen as harbinger of Antichrist, the
Arian, as it is called, considering that other heresies, her
elder sisters, have been openly proscribed, in her craft and
cunning, affects to array herself in Scripture language, like
her father the devil, and is forcing her way back into the
Church's paradise, — that with the pretence of Christianity,
her smooth sophistry (for reason she has none) may deceive
men into wrong thoughts of Christ.

Athanasius
c. 296-373

Most of Athanasius' life was spent in conflict with Arianism,
which involved not only the church but the political powers of
the Roman Empire as well. Athanasius refused to compromise
with Arianism and was exiled from Alexandria five times,
which led him to travel to Tyre, Rome, Antioch, Milan and the
deserts of Egypt. It is often said Athansius stood "against the

world" in his defense of the orthodox faith and that his steadfastness and even stubbornness helped the church overcome its enemies within and without. He lived his last few years in peace and even built the Memorial Church of Alexandria before his death.

more than the others. Some of his most famous works are *On the Incarnation of God*, *Against the Heathen* and the *Life of Antony*. He also wrote a history of Arianism including a sequel, *Against the Arians*.

SATURDAY, SECOND WEEK OF LENT

Holy Knowledge

Timothy, guard what has been entrusted to your care. Turn away from godless chatter and the opposing ideas of what is falsely called knowledge, which some have professed and in so doing have wandered from the faith. Grace be with you.
1 Timothy 6:20-21

Our Lord and Saviour, when He was persecuted by the Pharisees, wept for their destruction. He was injured, but He threatened not; not when He was afflicted, not even when He was killed. But He grieved for those who dared to do such things. He, the Saviour, suffered for man, but they despised and cast from them life, and light, and grace. All these were theirs through that Saviour Who suffered in our stead. And verily for their darkness and blindness, He wept. For if they had under-stood the things which are written in the Psalms, they would not have been so vainly daring against the Saviour, the Spirit having said, 'Why do the heathen rage, and the people imagine a vain thing?' And if they had considered the prophecy of Moses, they would not have hanged Him Who was their Life.

And if they had examined with their understanding the things which were written, they would not have carefully fulfilled the prophecies which were against themselves, so as for their city to be now desolate, grace taken from them, and they themselves without the law, being no longer called children, but strangers.

Athanasius
c. 296-373

This reading comes from a letter sent from Athanasius to Theodorus of Heliopolis in 338 A.D. on the subject of Easter. He has just returned from exile and has called together the bishops and elders of the Alexandrian area. Notice how Athanasius reflects on the attitude of Jesus Christ toward those who persecuted him. All Christians everywhere should imitate the same attitude in dealing with persecution, hardships, trouble and suffering.

THIRD SUNDAY OF LENT

Confession

This is the message we have heard from him and declare to you: God is light; in him there is no darkness at all. If we claim to have fellowship with him yet walk in the darkness, we lie and do not live by the truth. But if we walk in the light, as he is in the light, we have fellowship with one another, and the blood of Jesus, his Son, purifies us from all sin. If we claim to be without sin, we deceive ourselves and the truth is not in us. If we confess our sins, he is faithful and just and will forgive us our sins and purify us from all unrighteousness.
   1 John 1:5-9

Cramped is the dwelling of my soul; do Thou expand it, that Thou mayest enter in. It is in ruins, restore Thou it. There is that about it which must offend Thine eyes; I confess and know it, but who will cleanse it? or to whom shall I cry but to Thee? Cleanse me from my secret sins, O Lord, and keep Thy servant from those of other men. I believe, and therefore do I speak; Lord, thou knowest. Have I not confessed my transgressions unto Thee, O my God; and Thou hast put away the iniquity of my heart?
   Augustine
   c. 354-430

Augustine was bishop of Hippo in North Africa. He was born in Thogaste, Algeria, to an unbelieving father (Patricuis) and a very devoted Christian mother (Monica). His mother took him to church and enrolled him in theological studies as well as literature, rhetoric, Greek philosophy and Latin. He left his childhood faith during his teenage years being strongly influenced by a gang of youth men called the "Wreckers." At age 17, he took a concubine who bore him a son, Adeodatus (d. 389 A.D.). He was with the concubine for 15 years until he abandoned her for an arranged marriage set up by his mother, Monica. In the end he never did get married.

MONDAY, THIRD WEEK OF LENT

Progress

Everyone who has this hope in him purifies himself, just as he is pure. Everyone who sins breaks the law; in fact, sin is lawlessness. But if anyone obeys his word, God's love is truly made complete in him. This is how we know we are in him: Whoever claims to live in him must walk as Jesus did.
   1 John 2:3-6

I have therefore been at pains to rid myself of all baggage and garments which might impede my progress, in order that, obedient to the command and sustained by the help of Christ, I may swim, unhindered by any clothing for the flesh or care for the morrow, across the seas of this present life, which, swelling with waves and echoing with the barking of our sins, like the dogs of Scylla, separates between us and God. I do not boast that I have accomplished this: even if I might so boast, I would glory only in the Lord, whose it is to accomplish what it is our part to desire; but my soul is in earnest that the judgments of the Lord be her chief desire.
   Augustine
   c. 354-430

In 373 A.D., Aurelius Augustine read Cicero's *Hortensius*, and this sparked a move back to God. He was not satisfied with the Old Latin Bible so he began to study Manichaeanism. Mani (or Manes) was born in Persia around 216 A.D. and promoted an offshoot of Gnosticism based on dualism, secret truths and the eternal conflict between good and evil. The appeal to Augustine came from their strict discipline including vegetarianism. He stayed with the Manichees for nearly a decade before going through a crisis of faith. During this time he taught rhetoric in Carthage, Rome and Milan. It was in Milan that Augustine heard the good news of Jesus Christ in a fresh and inviting way from the preaching of Ambrose.

TUESDAY, THIRD WEEK OF LENT

Prayer

But you have an anointing from the Holy One, and all of you know the truth.
1 John 2:20-24

Pray for us: we value your prayers as worthy to be heard, since you go to God with so great an offering of unfeigned love, and of praise brought to Him by your works. Pray that in us also these works may shine, for He to whom you pray knows with what fullness of joy we behold them shining in you. Such are our desires; such are the abounding comforts which in the multitude of our thoughts within us delight our souls. It is so now because such is the promise of God; and as He hath promised, so shall it be in the time to come.

Augustine
c. 354-430

The first time Augustine went to hear Ambrose preach was not for spiritual reasons but because Ambrose was famous as an orator and held remarkable rhetorical powers. Later he went to church to hear the Word and not the words. He lost the belief in Mani's philosophy and suffered under the emotional strain of breaking up with his lifelong love. During the summer of 386 a.d. Augustine sat in a garden alone, reflecting on his life, when he read a passage from Romans on the kingdom of God. He made a decision to abandon his secular career and upcoming arranged marriage, and committed his life to Jesus Christ. He was baptized on Holy and Great Saturday (Easter eve) by Ambrose in Milan the very next year. The passage he read was: *Let us behave decently, as in the daytime, not in orgies and drunkenness, not in sexual immorality and debauchery, not in dissension and jealousy. Rather, clothe yourselves with the Lord Jesus Christ, and do not think about how to gratify the desires of the sinful nature* (Romans 13:13-14).

WEDNESDAY, THIRD WEEK OF LENT

Sacrifice

Two other men, both criminals, were also led out with him to be executed. When they came to the place called the Skull, there they crucified him, along with the criminals – one on his right, the other on his left.

One of the criminals who hung there hurled insults at him: "Aren't you the Christ? Save yourself and us!" But the other criminal rebuked him. "Don't you fear God," he said, "since you are under the same sentence? We are punished justly, for we are getting what our deeds deserve. But this man has done nothing wrong." Then he said, "Jesus, remember me when you come into your kingdom." Jesus answered him, "I tell you the truth, today you will be with me in paradise."

Luke 23:32-33; 39-43

Three crosses stood in one place: on one was the thief who was to be saved; on the second, the thief who was to be condemned; on the third, between them, was Christ, who was about to save the one thief and condemn the other. What could be more similar than these crosses? What more unlike than the persons who were suspended on them?

Augustine
c. 354-430

After his conversion, Augustine moved to Rome and in 388 A.D. buried his mother, Monica, in Ostia. He returned to North Africa and started a monastic community for laypeople. In 391 A.D. Augustine was ordained an elder against his wishes and placed in the service of Bishop Valerius of Hippo. In the summer of 395 A.D. Augustine became the bishop of Hippo and served there until his death on August 28, 430 A.D.

Augustine's most famous work, *Confessions*, was written three years after he became bishop. He detailed his early life, his abandonment of the faith, his embrace of Manichaeanism and his conversion to Jesus Christ, including his repentance of sin and worldly philosophy.

THURSDAY, THIRD WEEK OF LENT

Perseverance

*Consider it pure joy, my brothers, whenever you face trials of
many kinds, because you know that the testing of your faith
develops perseverance. Perseverance must finish its work so that
you may be mature and complete, not lacking anything. If any of
you lacks wisdom, he should ask God, who gives generously to all
without finding fault, and it will be given to him. But when he asks,
he must believe and not doubt, because he who doubts is like a
wave of the sea, blown and tossed by the wind. That man should
not think he will receive anything from the Lord; he is a double-
minded man, unstable in all he does.*
James 1:2-8

The belief of the resurrection of our Lord from the dead,
and of His ascension into heaven, has strengthened our faith
by adding a great buttress of hope. For it clearly shows how
freely He laid down His life for us when He had it in His
power thus to take it up again. With what assurance, then, is
the hope of believers animated, when they reflect how great
He was who suffered so great things for them while they
were still in unbelief!
Augustine
c. 354-430

Augustine opposed Donatism, which was a North African
controversy on the purity and holiness of the priests and
church leaders. The Donatists believed the church must be
"holy" and that any traitors to Christ or the kingdom of God
would invalidate their faith and infect the church. Augustine
counterattacked with the thought the validity of the church
(especially the sacraments) rested not on its priests or leaders,
but on Jesus Christ Who is the head of the church and the great
High Priest forever.

FRIDAY, THIRD WEEK OF LENT

Peace

Rejoice in the Lord always. I will say it again: Rejoice! Let your gentleness be evident to all. The Lord is near. Do not be anxious about anything, but in everything, by prayer and petition, with thanksgiving, present your requests to God. And the peace of God, which transcends all understanding, will guard your hearts and your minds in Christ Jesus.
Philippians 4:4-7

The peace of body and soul is the well-ordered and harmonious life and health of the living creature. Peace between man and God is the well-ordered obedience of faith to eternal law. Peace between man and man is well-ordered concord. Domestic peace is the well-ordered concord between those of the family who rule and those who obey. Civil peace is a similar concord among the citizens. The peace of the celestial city is the perfectly ordered and harmonious enjoyment of God, and of one another in God. The peace of all things is the tranquility of order. Order is the distribution which allots things equal and unequal, each to its own place.
Augustine
c. 354-430

Another famous work by Augustine is *The City of God,* written just before his death in 430 A.D. He describes the difference between a Christian empire and the eternal kingdom of God, and the responsibilities of the church to proclaim grace, truth and the forgiveness of sins through Jesus Christ. Augustine also wrote sermons and commentaries on the Gospels, Psalms, the Trinity and Christian doctrine. He wrote a rebuttal to Jerome's negative views on sex and marriage, and created a handbook on fourth-century theology. He strongly believed in taking the Gospel to the ends of the world, and produced several works in explaining the good news to a pagan audience. The sheer volume of his work and the fact that he has been read by the likes of Luther, Calvin, Wesley and others contributes to his continual popularity and usage. Augustine is held in high regard in the Roman Catholic, Eastern Orthodox and Protestant churches.

SATURDAY, THIRD WEEK OF LENT

Eternal Rest

Therefore, since the promise of entering his rest still stands, let us be careful that none of you be found to have fallen short of it. For we also have had the gospel preached to us, just as they did; but the message they heard was of no value to them, because those who heard did not combine it with faith.
Hebrews 4:1-2

But there is not now space to treat of these ages; suffice it to say that the seventh shall be our Sabbath, which shall be brought to a close, not by an evening, but by the Lord's day, as an eighth and eternal day, consecrated by the resurrection of Christ, and prefiguring the eternal repose not only of the spirit, but also of the body. There we shall rest and see, see and love, love and praise. This is what shall be in the end without end. For what other end do we propose to ourselves than to attain to the kingdom of which there is no end?
Augustine
c. 354-430

Augustine dealt with the very best and worst of his day. He defended the church from Gnosticism, Arianism, Mani's philosophy and the Pelagian controversy (a debate on the doctrine of original sin and humanity's freedom to choose good because of humanity's original image). He also criticized and exhorted the church to reform her ways, repent of her sins and put her faith solely in Jesus Christ. Grace was the key to Augustine's salvation, and he guarded that grace with great care.

Augustine's theology grew and changed over the years. When he was younger and wrote *Confessions*, he stressed free will and the prevenient grace of God. Throughout his debate with Pelagius he became more extreme in his view of election and predestination. In his last days he penned *The City of God*, which strongly stresses the eternal plan and purposes of God. This has led to a dichotomy of theology on eternal security with Wesleyans quoting the early Augustine and the Calvinists quoting the later Augustine. Maybe Augustine was right in his faith journey....

SUNDAY, FOURTH WEEK OF LENT

Great Grace

*During the days of Jesus' life on earth, he offered up prayers
and petitions with loud cries and tears to the one who could save
him from death, and he was heard because of his reverent submission. Although he was a son, he learned obedience from what he
suffered and, once made perfect, he became the source of eternal
salvation for all who obey him.*
   Hebrews 5:7-9

There stands the priest, not bringing down fire from
Heaven, but the Holy Spirit: and he makes prolonged
supplication, not that some flame sent down from on high
may consume the offerings, but that grace descending on the
sacrifice may thereby enlighten the souls of all, and render
them more refulgent than silver purified by fire. Who can
despise this most awful mystery, unless he is stark mad and
senseless? Or do you not know that no human soul could
have endured that fire in the sacrifice, but all would have
been utterly consumed, had not the assistance of God's grace
been great.
   John Chrysostom
   c. 347-407

John Chrysostom was the bishop of Constantinople and
considered a "Doctor of the Church" in both the Roman
Catholic and Eastern Orthodox churches. He was born in
Antioch and raised by his mother after his father died while he
was an infant. Anthusa (his mother) refused to remarry and
dedicated her time to educating John and his older sister. He
studied law first in Antioch and then later studied theology
under Diodore of Tarsus.

John wanted to live the monastic life but needed to take care of his mother, so he spent time at home in prayer, fasting and study. His strict discipline endangered his health. In 381 A.D. he was made a deacon and served under Bishop Flavian of Antioch. He was ordained an elder in 386 A.D. and sent to preach where he earned the nickname "Golden-Mouth" (Chrysostom). He preached several times in Antioch with revival and social reforms breaking out after his messages. A collection of his sermons are available from Genesis, Psalms, Isaiah, Matthew, John, Acts and the letters of Paul.

MONDAY, FOURTH WEEK OF LENT

Great Labor

*God is not unjust; he will not forget your work and the love
you have shown him as you have helped his people and continue to
help them. We want each of you to show this same diligence to the
very end, in order to make your hope sure. We do not want you to
become lazy, but to imitate those who through faith and patience
inherit what has been promised.*
Hebrews 6:10-12

For though the preacher may have great ability (and this
one would only find in a few), not even in this case is he
released from perpetual toil. For since preaching does not
come by nature, but by study, suppose a man to reach a high
standard of it, this will then forsake him if he does not culti-
vate his power by constant application and exercise. So that
there is greater labor for the wiser than for the unlearned.
John Chrysostom
c.347-407

John was made patriarch of Constantinople in 398 A.D. against
his will. He went there to the Roman capital of the Eastern
Empire to bring reform to the church and society. He felt the
pastors, church leaders, judges and politicians were caught up
in corruption, and that only the grace of God could deliver
them. He soon found the displeasure of the emperor and
empress and was exiled from the city three times.

John has his supporters as well. The people of Constantinople
loved him; many of the local pastors shared his views; and
even the bishop of Rome, Innocent I, tried to save him. His life
was in the hands of God. He sold all the costly furniture of the
episcopal palace and gave it to the poor; he donated his salary
to charity; he fasted and prayed, and required the clergy to do
the same; he refused invitations with the rich and famous; he

spoke out against the unjust rulings of the emperor and empress; he gave no dinner parties and exhorted the rich to almsgiving and simple living.

TUESDAY, FOURTH WEEK OF LENT

The Cross of Christ

The entire law is summed up in a single command: "Love your neighbor as yourself."
Galatians 5:14

For the cross destroyed the enmity of God towards man, brought about the reconciliation, made the earth Heaven, associated men with angels, pulled down the citadel of death, unstrung the force of the devil, extinguished the power of sin, delivered the world from error, brought back the truth, expelled the Demons, destroyed temples, over-turned altars, suppressed the sacrificial offering, implanted virtue, founded the Churches. The cross is the will of the Father, the glory of the Son, the rejoicing of the Spirit, the boast of Paul, "for," he says, "God forbid that I should boast save in the cross of our Lord Jesus Christ."
John Chrysostom
c. 347-407

John described his feelings about exile in a letter to Bishop Cyriacus: "When I was driven from the city, I felt no anxiety, but said to myself: If the empress wishes to banish me, let her do so; 'the earth is the Lord's.' If she wants to have me sawn asunder, I have Isaiah for an example. If she wants me to be drowned in the ocean, I think of Jonah. If I am to be thrown into the fire, the three men in the furnace suffered the same. If cast before wild beasts, I remember Daniel in the lion's den. If she wants me to be stoned, I have before me Stephen, the first martyr. If she demands my head, let her do so; John the Baptist shines before me. Naked I came from my mother's womb, naked shall I leave this world. Paul reminds me, 'If I still pleased men, I would not be the servant of Christ.'"

WEDNESDAY, FOURTH WEEK OF LENT

Spiritual Healing

Therefore confess your sins to each other and pray for each other so that you may be healed. The prayer of a righteous man is powerful and effective.
James 5:16

At length the season is verging towards the end of the Fast, and therefore we ought the more earnestly to devote ourselves to holiness. For as in the case of those who run a race, all their circuits will be of no avail if they miss the prize; so neither will any advantage result from these manifold labours and toils with regard to the fast, if we are not able to enjoy the sacred Table with a good conscience. For this end are fasting and Lent appointed, and so many days of solemn assemblies, auditories, prayers, and teachings, in order that by this earnestness being cleansed in every possible way from the sins which we had contracted during the whole year, we may with spiritual boldness religiously partake of that unbloody Sacrifice; so that should this not be the result, we shall have sustained so much labour entirely in vain, and without any profit.

John Chrysostom
c. 347-407

John served as the bishop of Constantinople from 398-404 A.D. and spent three years in exile.

He was first exiled to Pontus, but the people of Constantinople revolted around the palace, thus forcing the emperor to recall the bishop. He was removed the second time after preaching against idolatry and was dragged from the church on Holy and Great Saturday (Easter eve) 404 A.D. during the service of holy baptism. He was banished to eastern Turkey but kept correspondence with the church, friends and supporters. This infuriated the cruel empress, and she had John rearrested and sent to the Caucasus hills where he died during the journey. His last words were also his motto: "Glory be to God for all things. Amen."

THURSDAY, FOURTH WEEK OF LENT

Holy Advantage

And we know that in all things God works for the good of those who love him who have been called according to his purpose.
Romans 8:28

All these things then being considered, let us always give thanks to God who loveth man; not merely for our deliverance from these fearful evils, but for their being permitted to overtake us, — learning this from the divine Scriptures, as well as from the late events that have befallen us; that He ever disposes all things for our advantage, with that loving kindness which is His attribute, which God grant, that we may continually enjoy, and so may obtain the kingdom of heaven, in Christ Jesus our Lord; to whom be glory and dominion for ever and ever. Amen.

John Chrysostom
c. 347-407

John left a remarkable amount of writings in the Greek language, including books on the priesthood, marriage and baptism, more than 600 sermons and commentaries, letters, speeches and liturgy. His theology comes from his preaching and teaching where he proclaimed the grace of God for holiness, obedience and worship. He attracted large crowds wherever he spoke and even rebuked them when they responded with applause. He said, "You praise what I have said, and receive my exhortation with tumults of applause; but show your approbation by obedience; that is the only praise I seek." Of course they applauded his rebuke as well.

*Starting with tomorrow's reading the scriptures will be from the Songs of Ascent (Psalms 120-130). Traditionally these Psalms would have been recited on the way to Jerusalem for the celebration of a feast day or pilgrimage; Jerusalem was the highest place in southern Palestine and so the Songs of Ascent prepared the traveler to "rise up" and meet with God. [9]

Eugene H. Peterson has faithfully expounded on the themes of this section of Psalms in his book, *A Long Obedience in the Same Direction.* The following list comes from his study:

Psalm 120 Repentance
Psalm 121 Providence
Psalm 122 Worship
Psalm 123 Service
Psalm 124 Help
Psalm 125 Security
Psalm 126 Joy
Psalm 127 Work
Psalm 128 Happiness
Psalm 129 Perseverance
Psalm 130 Hope
Psalm 131 Humility
Psalm 132 Obedience
Psalm 133 Community
Psalm 134 Blessing [10]

FRIDAY, FOURTH WEEK OF LENT

Faith Journey

I call on the Lord in my distress, and he answers me. Save me, O Lord, from lying lips and from deceitful tongues.
Psalms 120:1-2

If all the members of my body were to be converted into tongues, and if each of my limbs were to be gifted with a human voice, I could still do no justice to the virtues of the holy and venerable Paula. Noble in family, she was nobler still in holiness; rich formerly in this world's goods, she is now more distinguished by the poverty that she has embraced for Christ. Of the stock of the Gracchi and descended from the Scipios, the heir and representative of that Paulus whose name she bore, the true and legitimate daughter of that Martia Papyria who was mother to Africanus, she yet preferred Bethlehem to Rome, and left her palace glittering with gold to dwell in a mud cabin. We do not grieve that we have lost this perfect woman; rather we thank God that we have had her, nay that we have her still. For "all live unto" God, and they who return unto the Lord are still to be reckoned members of his family. We have lost her, it is true, but the heavenly mansions have gained her; for as long as she was in the body she was absent from the Lord.

Jerome
c. 345-420

Jerome studied in Rome where he confessed his faith in Jesus Christ and was baptized. He traveled to Gaul and devoted his life to prayer and fasting. In 374 A.D. he went to Palestine and stayed in Antioch before living in the Syrian desert for five years. He was ordained an elder before heading back to Rome to serve as the secretary to the bishop of Rome. In 386 A.D. he settled in Bethlehem where he started a monastery and spent time in solitude and study.

SATURDAY, FOURTH WEEK OF LENT

Holy Living

I rejoiced with those who said to me, "Let us go to the house of the Lord." Our feet are standing in your gates, O Jerusalem. The Lord will keep you from all harm – he will watch over your life; the Lord will watch over your coming and going both now and forevermore.

Psalms 121:1-2; 7-8

You urge me to revise the old Latin version, and, as it were, to sit in judgment on the copies of the Scriptures which are now scattered throughout the whole world; and, inasmuch as they differ from one another, you would have me decide which of them agree with the Greek original. The labour is one of love, but at the same time both perilous and presumptuous; for in judging others I must be content to be judged by all; and how can I dare to change the language of the world in its hoary old age, and carry it back to the early days of its infancy?

Jerome

c. 345-420

Jerome's greatest work was his translation of the early Greek manuscripts of the New Testament into the Latin Vulgate. He did this while serving Bishop Damasus of Rome. He started with the Gospels and then went to the Psalms. He spent nearly 15 years just on the Old Testament alone. His translation of the entire Bible received criticism both then and throughout history. It is generally accepted that his work was excellent although not without some faults.

He also wrote commentaries and left many letters on spiritual direction, prayer and worship. He enjoyed debating the issues of his day, and his contemporaries like Augustine and Rufinus rebuked more than once. Jerome even met Pelagius in Rome and was drawn by his simplicity. He described him as a "big man who moved like a turtle."

SUNDAY, FIFTH WEEK OF LENT

True Disciples of Christ

Pray for the peace of Jerusalem: May those who love you be secure.
Psalms 122:6

There are some who call themselves Christian, and who attend worship regularly, yet perform no Christian actions in their daily lives. There are others who do not call themselves Christian, and who never attend worship, yet perform many Christian actions in their daily lives. Which of these two groups are the better disciples of Christ? Some would say that believing in Christ and worshipping him is what matters for salvation. But this is not what Jesus himself said. His teaching was almost entirely concerned with action, and with the motives which inspire action. He affirmed goodness of behaviour in whoever he found, whether the person was Jew or Roman, male or female. And he condemned those who kept all the religious requirements, yet were greedy and cruel. Jesus does not invite people to become his disciples for his own benefit, but to teach and guide them in the ways of goodness. And if a person can walk along that way without ever knowing the earthly Jesus, then we may say that he is following the spirit of Christ in his heart.

Pelagius
c. 354-430

Pelagius was born in Wales and converted in Britain under the influence of Celtic Christians. He studied theology and was fluent in Greek and Latin but was never ordained. He devoted his life to prayer and fasting and engaged in spiritual direction before going to Rome around 380 A.D.

He became friends with Celestius and traveled to Palestine and Africa where they taught that humanity could seek salvation by its own efforts apart from God's grace. They were condemned at the Council of Carthage in 411 A.D. and declared "heretics." Augustine, who labored long to defeat Pelagianism, had once admired Pelagius and referred to him as a "saintly man." The debate continued for several decades but Pelagius himself disappeared from the public scene. Celestius continued to appeal for reinstatement up until the Council of Ephesus in 431 A.D. Semipelagianism was developed to contradict Augustine's later writings on extreme predestination and still produces heated debates in modern theological discussions.

MONDAY, FIFTH WEEK OF LENT

Faith and Mercy

*Have mercy on us, O Lord, have mercy on us, for we have
endured much contempt.*
Psalms 123:3

Sailors at night are cheered by the sight of the harbour
lights, and so are they who are in peril for the sake of the
apostolic faith by the zeal of them that share the faith. We
have great comfort in what we hear of your godliness's
efforts on behalf of the divine doctrines, for this mind has
been given you by the Giver of all good gifts and for the safe
keeping of these doctrines you undergo every toil. Now I,
comforted by your zeal, make an insignificant return, calling
on you to persevere in your divine labours, to despise your
adversaries as an easy prey, (for what is weaker than they
who are destitute of the truth?) and to trust in Him who said
"I will not fail thee nor forsake thee," and "Lo I am with you
always even unto the end of the world."
Theodoret
c. 393-460

Theodoret was bishop of Cyrrhus in Syria. He was born in
Antioch and educated in a monastic school before entering the
monastery in 416 A.D. He was consecrated bishop against his
will in 433 A.D. but led his flock with wisdom, grace and love.

He battled Apollinarianism during his pastoral service and tried
to emphasize the humanity of Christ. Apollinarus (c. 310-390)
taught that Christ did not have a human mind, soul and will,
and was condemned by the Council of Constantinople in
381 A.D. He later left the church and went on his own.

Theodoret suffered exile for his defense of Christ but later was
recalled and spent the last years of his life preaching and

teaching in peace. Only a few fragments of his work remain, including several treaties on the divine and human natures of Christ. Most of his biblical commentaries deal with the Old Testament, especially the prophets.

TUESDAY, FIFTH WEEK OF LENT

Pleasing God

If the Lord had not been on our side let Israel say — if the Lord had not been on our side when men attacked us, when their anger flared against us, they would have swallowed us alive; the flood would have engulfed us, the torrent would have swept over us, the raging waters would have swept us away. Praise be to the Lord, who has not let us be torn by their teeth. We have escaped like a bird out of the fowler's snare; the snare has been broken, and we have escaped. Our help is in the name of the Lord, the Maker of heaven and earth.

Psalms 124:1-8

The lesson also which was read today invites you to the true faith, by setting before you the way in which you also must please God: for it affirms that without faith it is impossible to please Him. For when will a man resolve to serve God, unless he believes that He is a giver of reward? When will a young woman choose a virgin life, or a young man live soberly, if they believe not that for chastity there is a crown that fadeth not away? Faith is an eye that enlightens every conscience, and imparts understanding.

Cyril of Jerusalem
c. 315-387

Cyril was bishop of Jerusalem and born into a Christian family around Palestine in 315 A.D. He was very familiar with the Holy Land before Constantine sent Helena there to locate the cross of Christ. He was ordained a deacon in 334 A.D. and later became an elder before becoming bishop in 350 A.D.

He stood against the Arians and was exiled twice from his church. Both Basil the Great and Gregory of Nyssa visited Cyril and reported that his faith was true, but that the church in

Jerusalem was full of factions and quarreling. Cyril himself sold everything he had to give to the poor and was often accused of not having proper attire for a bishop.

WEDNESDAY, FIFTH WEEK OF LENT

Abiding Faith

Those who trust in the Lord are like Mount Zion, which cannot be shaken but endures forever. As the mountains surround Jerusalem, so the Lord surrounds his people both now and forevermore.
Psalms 125:1-2

Since then we have the prophecies, let faith abide with us. Let them fall who fall through unbelief, since they so will; but thou hast taken thy stand on the rock of the faith in the Resurrection. Let no heretic ever persuade thee to speak evil of the Resurrection. For to this day the Manichees say, that, the resurrection of the Saviour was phantom-wise, and not real, not heeding Paul who says, Who was made of the seed of David according to the flesh; and again, By the resurrection of Jesus Christ our Lord from the dead. And again he aims at them, and speaks thus, Say not in thine heart, who shall ascend into heaven; or who shall descend into the deep? that is, to bring up Christ from the dead; and in like manner warning as he has elsewhere written again, Remember Jesus Christ raised from the dead; and again, And if Christ be not risen, then is our preaching vain, and your faith also vain.
Cyril of Jerusalem
c. 315-387

Cyril left a series of discipleship training materials that were used for new Christians seeking baptism. He stressed the "real presence" of the Lord in the life of the believer and required all new Christians to attend the classes. They were taught the Nicene Creed followed by the Lord's Prayer. Specific instruction was given on illumination, repentance, confession and exorcism, which prepared the new Christians for baptism. At their baptism they renounced evil; professed their faith in Jesus

Christ; received anointing for the Holy Spirit; cleansed with water (baptism); and were blessed for spiritual gifts and graces. This became the standard for baptism in the Roman Catholic and Eastern Orthodox churches.

THURSDAY, FIFTH WEEK OF LENT

Becoming

The Lord has done great things for us, and we are filled with joy. Restore our fortunes, O Lord, like streams in the Negev. Those who sow in tears will reap with songs of joy. He who goes out weeping, carrying seed to sow, will return with songs of joy, carrying sheaves with him.
   Psalms 126:3-6

Let us become like Christ, since Christ became like us. Let us become God's for His sake, since He for ours became Man. He assumed the worse that He might give us the better; He became poor that we through His poverty might be rich; He took upon Him the form of a servant that we might receive back our liberty; He came down that we might be exalted; He was tempted that we might conquer; He was dishonoured that He might glorify us; He died that He might save us; He ascended that He might draw to Himself us, who were lying low in the Fall of sin. Let us give all, offer all, to Him Who gave Himself a Ransom and a Reconciliation for us. But one can give nothing like oneself, understanding the Mystery, and becoming for His sake all that He became for ours.
   Gregory of Nazianzus
   c. 329-390

Gregory of Nazianzus was one of the Cappadocian Fathers (Basil the Great, Gregory of Nazianzus and Gregory of Nyssa) and is known as "Gregory the Theologian." He grew up in Cappadocia where his father was bishop, but studied in Athens where he met Basil. He was ordained an elder in 362 A.D. against his will and consecrated as the bishop of Sasima where he never actually resided. He chose to remain in Cappadocia to help his father until his father's death in 374 A.D.

He retired to live a life of prayer and study but was called to Constantinople to help prepare for the Council of 381 A.D. He was appointed bishop of Constantinople but resigned and went home to live his final years in prayer.

FRIDAY, FIFTH WEEK OF LENT

Unbounded

Unless the Lord builds the house, its builders labor in vain.
Unless the Lord watches over the city, the watchmen stand guard
in vain. In vain you rise early and stay up late, toiling for food to
eat — for he grants sleep to those he loves. Sons are a heritage
from the Lord, children a reward from him. Like arrows in the
hands of a warrior are sons born in one's youth. Blessed is the
man whose quiver is full of them. They will not be put to shame
when they contend with their enemies in the gate.
Psalms 127:1-5

God always was, and always is, and always will be. Or
rather, God always Is. For Was and Will be are fragments of
our time, and of changeable nature, but He is Eternal Being.
And this is the Name that He gives to Himself when giving
the Oracle to Moses in the Mount. For in Himself He sums
up and contains all Being, having neither beginning in the
past nor end in the future; like some great Sea of Being,
limitless and unbounded, transcending all conception of
time and nature, only adumbrated by the mind, and that
very dimly and scantily....
Gregory of Nazianzus
c. 329-390

Gregory's writings include *The Five Theological Orations*, which
defends the doctrine of the Trinity and won him the title of
"Theologian." He also left sermons and treaties on a variety of
subjects like the peace of God, judgment, poverty, marriage,
character and holiness. He wrote orations about the death of
his father and his sister, and penned 507 poems. Here is an
example:
O Word of God and Light and Life and Wisdom and Might
for I rejoice in all Thy names

O offspring and Expression and Signet of the Great Mind;
O Word conceived and Man contemplated, who bearest
  all things,
binding them by the Word of Thy power receive
  this discourse.

SATURDAY, FIFTH WEEK OF LENT

Drawing Near

May the Lord bless you from Zion all the days of your life;
may you see the prosperity of Jerusalem, and may you live to see
your children's children. Peace be upon Israel.
Psalms 128:5-6

We confessed that the Christ Who was manifested is very
God, as much before as after our sojourn at Jerusalem; our
faith in Him was not increased afterwards any more than it
was diminished. Before we saw Bethlehem we knew His
being made man by means of the Virgin; before we saw His
Grave we believed in His Resurrection from the dead; apart
from seeing the Mount of Olives, we confessed that His
Ascension into heaven was real. We derived only thus much
of profit from our travelling thither, namely that we came to
know by being able to compare them, that our own places are
far holier than those abroad. Wherefore, O ye who fear the
Lord, praise Him in the places where ye now are. Change of
place does not effect any drawing nearer unto God, but
wherever thou mayest be, God will come to thee, if the
chambers of thy soul be found of such a sort that He can
dwell in thee and walk in thee.

Gregory of Nyssa
c. 330-395

Gregory was bishop of Nyssa and was the younger brother to
Basil the Great. He was raised around Asia Minor in a Christian home with nine brothers and sisters. His father died when
he was young, and his mother, Emmelia, and grandmother
Macrina took care of the children. He showed an interest in
rhetoric but answered the call of God on his life to be a pastor.
Emmelia had urged him to come to a worship service honoring

Christian martyrs, and later that night he dreamed that the martyrs had a special message for him.

He was a married pastor (wife — Theosabeia) and was made bishop in 371 A.D. He defended the faith against the Arians and was disposed in 376 A.D. but returned two years later.

PALM SUNDAY

Triumphal Entry

May those who pass by not say, 'The blessing of the Lord be upon you; we bless you in the name of the Lord.'
Psalms 129:8

And if you have so gladdened us, by only sending us the joyful tidings of your coming, that everything changed for us from extremest woe to a bright condition, what will your precious and benign coming, even the sight of it, do? What consolation will the sound of your sweet voice in our ears afford our soul? May this speedily come to pass, by the good help of God, Who giveth respite from pain to the fainting, and rest to the afflicted. But be assured, that when we look at our own case we grieve exceedingly at the present state of things, and men cease not to tear us in pieces: but when we turn our eyes to your excellence, we own that we have great cause for thankfulness to the dispensation of Divine Providence, that we are able to enjoy in your neighbourhood your sweetness and good-will towards us, and feast at will. ...

Gregory of Nyssa
c. 330-395

Gregory was a good thinker and theologian using ideas he learned from Greek philosophy, Origen and Holy Scripture. He wrote articles against Apollinarianism, Arianism and Eunomius. He promoted the Trinity, virginity, faith, pilgrimages and defended the Nicene dogma. He also taught that Mary was truly theotokos or the "bearer of God the Son."

He was very close to his sister Macrina, who was named after their grandmother, and wrote a biography of her life and faith. He also used her in his book *On the Soul and the Resurrection* in which they questioned each other on life after death and the nature of the eternal resurrection.

This passage comes from a letter to a friend on the presence of God refreshing the soul. He says earlier: "In the multitude of the sorrows which I had in my heart, the comforts of God, by your kindness, have refreshed my soul."

HOLY MONDAY

Knowledge or Faith

I wait for the Lord, my soul waits, and in his word I put my hope.
Psalms 130:5

Which is first in order, knowledge or faith? I reply that generally, in the case of disciples, faith precedes knowledge. But, in our teaching, if any one asserts knowledge to come before faith, I make no objection; understanding knowledge so far as is within the bounds of human comprehension. In our lessons we must first believe that the letter a is said to us; then we learn the characters and their pronunciation, and the last of all we get the distinct idea of the force of the letter. But in our belief about God, first comes the idea that God is. This we gather from His works. For, as we perceive His wisdom, His goodness, and all His invisible things from the creation of the world, so we know Him. So, too, we accept Him as our Lord. For since God is the Creator of the whole world, and we are a part of the world, God is our Creator. This knowledge is followed by faith, and this faith by worship.

Basil the Great
c. 330-379

Basil the Great was bishop of Caesarea and the brother to Gregory of Nyssa and Macrina. His mother, Emmelia, and grandmother Macrina raised him and his nine siblings after his father died. He was educated in Constantinople and Athens where he became friends with Gregory of Nazianzus, and together with Gregory of Nyssa emerged as the Cappadocian Fathers. He spent time as a hermit in Syria and Egypt developing his faith through prayer, fasting and solitude. He often went on preaching missions with Gregory of Nazianzus. Basil left the monastic life to defend the faith against the

Arian emperor, Volens, at the request of Eusebius of Caesarea in 364 A.D. He was later appointed bishop of Caesarea after Eusebius died.

HOLY TUESDAY

Coming Home

My heart is not proud, O Lord, my eyes are not haughty; I do not concern my self with great matters or things too wonderful for me. But I have tilled and quieted my soul; like a weaned child with its mother, like a weaned child is my soul within me. I will not enter my house or go to my bed.
Psalms 131:1-3

If, then, the sojourn of the Lord in flesh had never taken place, the Redeemer paid not the fine to death on our behalf, nor through Himself destroyed death's reign. For if what was reigned over by death was not that which was assumed by the Lord, death would not have ceased working his own ends, nor would the sufferings of the God-bearing flesh have been made our gain; He would not have killed sin in the flesh; we who had died in Adam should not have been made alive in Christ; the fallen to pieces would not have been set up again; that which by the serpent's trick had been estranged from God would never have been made once more His own.

Basil the Great
c. 330-379

Basil's most famous literary work came when he was defending the doctrine of the Trinity. His book *On the Holy Spirit* taught that the Holy Spirit was divine and very much a part of the Godhead. He also edited a collection of works from Origen with Gregory of Nazianzus. He always listened to all the sides during debate and tried to bring reconciliation to several disputers including the Semiarians (over the Nicene Creed); Apollinarians (over Christiology) and of course, the Arians (over the nature of Christ).

He also left a wealth of writings on the monastic life including the *Rule of Basil*. These 80 rules were based on the New Testament to help disciples in worship, work and faith sharing. He used a question-and-answer format, which applied the rules to the monastic community.

HOLY WEDNESDAY

Capacity of Faith

"Let us go to his dwelling place; let us worship at his foot-stool — arise, O Lord, and come to your resting place, you and the ark of your might. May your priests be clothed with righteousness; may your saints sing for joy." For the sake of David your servant, do not reject your anointed one.
Psalms 132:7-10

But among others the unfathomable depth of Christ's beneficence was so stopped up, that it was said: "And Jesus could do there no mighty works because of their unbelief." And so the bounty of God is actually shaped according to the capacity of man's faith, so that to one it is said: "According to thy faith be it unto thee:" and to another: "Go thy way, and as thou hast believed so be it unto thee;" to another "Be it unto thee according as thou wilt," and again to another: "Thy faith hath made thee whole."

John Cassian
c. 360-430

John Cassian was a monk born in Scytha Minor and sent to a monastery near Bethlehem at an early age. He studied in Egypt and eventually traveled to Constantinople where he was ordained a deacon in the service of John Chrysostom. He visited Rome and founded two monasteries in France where he remained the rest of his life.

He wrote two books on monastic living, *Institutes* and *Conferences*, which set down rules for the community of faith and gives testimony from monks on their growth in grace. John believed there were eight hindrances to holiness, which later developed into the seven deadly sins: pride; greed; lust; envy; gluttony; anger; and sloth. John's eighth hindrance was "acedia," which was combined with "sloth." He thought sloth to be more along the lines of "laziness" or "negligence," and acedia to be "indifference" or "restlessness." He suggested that acedia could be avoided by regular times of prayer and spiritual conversations with another Christ follower.

MAUNDY THURSDAY

Eternal Bread

How good and pleasant it is when brothers live together in unity! It is like precious oil poured on the head, running down on the beard, running down on Aaron's beard, down upon the collar of his robes. It is as if the dew of Hermon were falling on Mount Zion. For there the Lord bestows his blessing, even life forevermore.
Psalms 133:1-3

We have proved the sacraments of the Church to be the more ancient, now recognize that they are superior. In every truth it is a marvelous thing that God rained manna on the fathers, and fed them with daily food from heaven; so that it is said, "So man did eat angels' food." But yet all those who ate that food died in the wilderness, but that food which you receive, that living Bread which came down from heaven, furnishes the substance of eternal life; and whosoever shall eat of this Bread shall never die, and it is the Body of Christ.
Ambrose
c. 339-397

Ambrose was bishop of Milan and born in Gaul. His father served in the Roman government, and Ambrose trained to be a public administrator and lawyer. He was appointed governor of a small area near Milan and was quite successful in civil affairs.

When Auxentius, bishop of Milan, died in 374 A.D., the city demanded that Ambrose be the next bishop. The problem was that he was still a new Christian and had not even been baptized. At first he resisted, but then consented to be baptized and ordained as an elder and started to study theology. He was a famous preacher bringing out the practical aspects of the faith. He also used his public-service experience to help organize and administrate the churches of Northern Italy. Most of his writing centered on Christian ethics and basic instructions for new believers. He helped lead Augustine to Christ and is considered to be one of the four traditional "Doctors of the Latin Church" along with Jerome, Augustine and Gregory the Great (sixth century).

GOOD FRIDAY

Obedience to the Cross

*Praise the Lord, all you servants of the Lord who minister by
night in the house of the Lord. Lift up your hands in the sanctuary
and praise the Lord. May the Lord, the Maker of heaven and earth,
bless you from Zion.*
    Psalms 134:1-3

*It was now about the sixth hour, and darkness came over the
whole land until the ninth hour, for the sun stopped shining. And
the curtain of the temple was torn in two. Jesus called out with a
loud voice, "Father, into your hands I commit my spirit." When he
had said this, he breathed his last. The centurion, seeing what had
happened, praised God and said, "Surely this was a righteous
man." When all the people who had gathered to witness this sight
saw what took place, they beat their breasts and went away. But all
those who knew him, including the women who had followed him
from Galilee, stood at a distance, watching these things.*
    Luke 23:44-49

For the Only-begotten Son of God was not cut off by
death. It is true that in order to take the whole of our nature
upon Him He submitted to death, that is to the apparent
severance of soul and body, and made His way even to the
realms below, the debt which man must manifestly pay: but
He rose again and abides for ever and looks down with an
eye that death cannot dim upon His enemies, being exalted
unto the glory of God and born once more Son of God after
becoming Son of Man, as He had been Son of God when He
first became Son of Man, by the glory of His resurrection.
    Hilary of Poitiers
    c. 315-368

Hilary was bishop of Poitiers and famous for writing hymns and songs of praise. He was converted from paganism and after being consecrated as a bishop, defended the faith against Arianism. He was exiled for four years but continued to write articles on the Trinity, commentaries on Matthew and Psalms, and a collection of books on church history.

HOLY AND GREAT SATURDAY

Lenten Prayer

Trust in the Lord with all your heart and lean not on your own understanding; in all your ways acknowledge him, and he will make your paths straight.
Proverbs 3:5-6

For Christ died for sins once for all, the righteous for the unrighteous, to bring you to God. He was put to death in the body but made alive by the Spirit, through whom also he went and preached to the spirits in prison who disobeyed long ago when God waited patiently in the days of Noah while the ark was being built. In it only a few people, eight in all, were saved through water, and this water symbolizes baptism that now saves you also — not the removal of dirt from the body but the pledge of a good conscience toward God. It saves you by the resurrection of Jesus Christ, who has gone into heaven and is at God's right hand — with angels, authorities and powers in submission to him.
1 Peter 3:18-22

O Lord and Master of my life,
take from me the spirit of sloth,
despair, lust of power and idle talk;
grant rather the spirit of chastity, humility,
patience and love to thy servant.
Yea, O Lord and King,
grant me to see my own transgressions
and not to judge my brother,
for blessed art Thou unto ages of ages.
Amen.
Ephraem Syrus
c. 306-373

Ephraem Syrus (the Syrian) was an ordained deacon and hymn writer in Syria and Persia. He was raised in a pagan home, but his family was converted to Jesus Christ, and he became a local worship leader. He traveled to Edessa and Egypt and was regarded for his holy living.

This "Lenten Prayer" is to be recited three times a day with reflection on the Lordship of Jesus Christ (line 1); repentance and transformation (lines 2-5); revelation (line 7); and mercy (line 8). It is still used today in Eastern Orthodox churches during the season of Lent.

RESURRECTION SUNDAY

Life

At that time Michael, the great prince who protects your people, will arise. There will be a time of distress such as has not happened from the beginning of nations until then. But at that time your people — everyone whose name is found written in the book — will be delivered. Multitudes who sleep in the dust of the earth will awake: some to everlasting life, others to shame and everlasting contempt. Those who are wise will shine like the brightness of the heavens, and those who lead many to righteousness, like the stars forever and ever.
Daniel 12:1-3

And if the Spirit of him who raised Jesus from the dead is living in you, he who raised Christ from the dead will also give life to your mortal bodies through his Spirit, who lives in you.
Romans 8:11

This is the Son of the carpenter, Who skillfully made His cross a bridge over Sheol that swallows up all, and brought over mankind into the dwelling of life. And because it was through the tree that mankind had fallen into Sheol, so upon the tree they passed over into the dwelling of life. Through the tree then wherein bitterness was tasted, through it also sweetness was tasted; that we might learn of Him that amongst the creatures nothing resists Him. Glory be to Thee, Who didst lay Thy cross as a bridge over death, that souls might Passover upon it from the dwelling of the dead to the dwelling of life!
Ephraem Syrus
c. 306-373

Ephraem left volumes of hymns, song and poems dedicated to the praise and worship of God. He often wrote on faith, paradise, hell and the saving power of Christ. He also produced articles defending the faith in the Latin, Greek and Syriac languages.

EASTER MONDAY

Cornerstone of Faith

On the evening of that first day of the week, when the disciples were together, with the doors locked for fear of the Jews, Jesus came and stood among them and said, "Peace be with you!" After he said this, he showed them his hands and side. The disciples were overjoyed when they saw the Lord.
John 20:19-20

Faith is compounded of many things, and by many kinds is it brought to perfection. For it is like a building that is built up of many pieces of workmanship and so its edifice rises to the top. And know, my beloved, that in the foundations of the building stones are laid, and so resting upon stones the whole edifice rises until it is perfected. Thus also the true Stone, our Lord Jesus Christ, is the foundation of all our faith. And on Him, on [this] Stone faith is based. And resting on faith all the structure rises until it is completed. For it is the foundation that is the beginning of all the building. For when any one is brought nigh unto faith, it is laid for him upon the Stone, that is our Lord Jesus Christ. And his building cannot be shaken by the waves, nor can it be injured by the winds. By the stormy blasts it does not fall, because its structure is reared upon the rock of the true Stone. And in this that I have called Christ the Stone, I have not spoken of my own thought, but the Prophets beforehand called Him the Stone. And this I shall make clear to thee.

Aphrahat
d. 415

Aphrahat is considered the first of the Syriac Church Fathers for writing 23 Demonstrations on faith, love, fasting, prayer, repentance and humilty. He called himself a "Disciple of the

Scriptures" and served the church in Syria during a time of
persecution and turmoil.

ENDNOTES

1 Johnson, Jeffrey P., *Emerging Faith Lenten Devotions* (Indianapolis, Indiana: Light and Life Communications, 2009).

2 Shelley, Bruce L., *Church History in Plain Language* (Nashville, Tennessee: Thomas Nelson Publishers, 1982) 29-35.

3 Maas, Robin and O'Donnell, O.P. Gabriel, *Spiritual Traditions for the Contemporary Church* (Nashville, Tennessee: Abingdon Press, 1990) 26-28.

4 Culbertson, Philip L. and Shippee, Arthur Bradford, *The Pastor: Readings from the Patristic Period* (Minneapolis, Minnesota: Fortress Press, 1990) 10-12.

5 Ibid., 13.

6 Jones, Cheslyn and Wainwright, Geoffrey and Yarnold, Sr. Edward, *The Study of Spirituality* (New York, New York: Oxford University Press, 1986) 120-121.

7 Robin and Gabriel, 38-39.

8 Shelley, 73.

9 Peterson, Eugene H., *A Long Obedience in the Same Direction: Discipleship in an Instant Society.* (Downers Grove: InterVarsity Press, 1980) 14.

10 Peterson, Eugene H., *A Long Obedience in the Same Direction: Discipleship in an Instant Society.* Downers Grove, Illinois: InterVarsity Press, 1980.

BIBLIOGRAPHY

Clement, Olivier. *Three Prayers: The Lord's Prayer, O Heavenly King, Prayer of St. Ephrem*. Crestwood, New York: St Vladimir's Seminary Press, 2000.

Culbertson, Philip L. and Shippee, Arthur Bradford, *The Pastor: Readings from the Patristic Period*. Minneapolis, Minnesota: Fortress Press, 1990.

Johnson, Jeffrey P., *Emerging Faith Lenten Devotions*. Indianapolis, Indiana: Light and Life Communications, 2009.

Jones, Cheslyn and Wainwright, Geoffrey and Yarnold, SJ, Edward. *The Study of Spirituality*. New York, New York: Oxford University Press, 1986.

Maas, Robin and O'Donnell, O.P. Gabriel, *Spiritual Traditions for the Contemporary Church*. Nashville, Tennessee: Abingdon Press, 1990.

Newell, J. Philip. *Listening for the Heartbeat of God: A Celtic Spirituality*. Mahwah, New Jersey: Paulist Press.

Peterson, Eugene H. *A Long Obedience in the Same Direction: Discipleship in an Instant Society*. Downers Grove: InterVarsity Press, 1980.

Roberts, Alexander, D.D., Donaldson, James, LL.D., *The Writings of the Fathers Down to A.D. 325, Volume 7, Lactantius, Venantius, Asterius, Victonius, Dionysius, Apostolic Teaching and Constitutions, 2 Clement, Early Liturgies*. Peabody, Massachusetts: Hendrickson Publishing, Inc, 1994.

Roberts, Alexander, D.D., Donaldson, James, LL.D., *The Writings of the Fathers Down to A.D. 325, Volume 8, The Twelve Patriarchs, Excerpts and Epistles, The Clementina, Apocrypha, Decretals, Memoirs of Edessa and Syriac Documents, Remains of the First Ages*. Peabody, Massachusetts: Hendrickson Publishing, Inc., 1994.

Shelley, Bruce L., *Church History in Plain Language*. Nashville, Tennessee: Thomas Nelson Publishers, 1982.

Schaff, Philip D.D., LL.D., *A Select Library of Nicene and Post-Nicene Fathers of the Christian Church, Volume 1, The Confessions and Letters of St. Augustine With a Sketch of His Life and Work, First Series*. Grand Rapids, Michigan: Wm. B. Eerdmans Publishing Company, 2001.

Schaff, Philip D.D., LL.D., *A Select Library of Nicene and Post-Nicene Fathers of the Christian Church, Volume 2, First Series. St. Augustine's: City of God and Christian Doctrine*. Grand Rapids, Michigan: Wm. B. Eerdmans Publishing Company, 1997.

Schaff, Philip D.D., LL.D. and Henry Wace, D.D., *A Select Library of Nicene and Post-Nicene Fathers of the Christian Church, Volume 1,*

Second Series. Eusebius: Church History, Life of Constantine the Great, Oration in Praise of Constantine. Grand Rapids, Michigan: Wm. B. Eerdmans Publishing Company, 1997.

Schaff, Philip D.D., LL.D. and Henry Wace, D.D., *A Select Library of Nicene and Post-Nicene Fathers of the Christian Church, Volume 2, Second Series. Socrates, Sozomenus: Church Histories.* Grand Rapids, Michigan: Wm. B. Eerdmans Publishing Company, 1997.

Schaff, Philip D.D., LL.D. and Henry Wace, D.D., *A Select Library of Nicene and Post-Nicene Fathers of the Christian Church, Volume 3, Theodoret, Jerome, Gennadius, Rufinus: Historical Writings, etc.* Grand Rapids, Michigan: Wm. B. Eerdmans Publishing Company, 1996.

Schaff, Philip D.D., LL.D. and Henry Wace, D.D., *A Select Library of Nicene and Post-Nicene Fathers of the Christian Church, Volume 4, Second Series Anthanasius: Select Works and Letters.* Grand Rapids, Michigan: Wm. B. Eerdmans Publishing Company, 1994.

Schaff, Philip D.D., LL.D. and Henry Wace, D.D., *A Select Library of the Christian Church Nicene and Post-Nicene Fathers of the Christian Church, Volume 5, Gregory of Nyssa: Dogmatic Treatises, etc. Second Series.* Grand Rapids, Michigan: Wm. B. Eerdmans Publishing Company, 1994.

Schaff, Philip D.D., LL.D. and Henry Wace, D.D., *A Select Library of Nicene and Post-Nicene Fathers of the Christian Church, Volume 6, St. Jerome: Letters and Select Works.* Grand Rapids, Michigan: Wm. B. Eerdmans Publishing Company, 1996.

Schaff, Philip D.D., LL.D. and Henry Wace, D.D., *A Select Library of Nicene and Post-Nicene Fathers of the Christian Church, Volume 7, Second Series S. Cyril of Jerusalem, S. Gregory Nazianzen.* Grand Rapids, Michigan: Wm. B. Eerdmans Publishing Company, 1996.

Schaff, Philip D.D., LL.D. and Henry Wace, D.D., *A Select Library of the Christian Church Nicene and Post-Nicene Fathers of the Christian Church, Volume 8, St. Basil: Letters and Select Works Second Series.* Grand Rapids, Michigan: Wm. B. Eerdmans Publishing Company, 1996.

Schaff, Philip D.D., LL.D., *A Select Library of Nicene and Post-Nicene Fathers of the Christian Church, Volume 9, St. Chrysostom: On the Priesthood; Ascetic Treaties; Homilies and Letters; Homilies on the Statues.* Grand Rapids, Michigan: Wm. B. Eerdmans Publishing Company, 1996.

Schaff Philip, D.D., LL.D. and Henry Wace, D.D., *A Select Library of Nicene and Post-Nicene Fathers of the Christian Church, Volume 9, St. Hilary of Poitiers, John of Damascus.* Grand Rapids, Michigan: Wm. B. Eerdmans Publishing Company, 1997.

Schaff, Philip D.D., LL.D. and Henry Wace, D.D., *A Select Library of Nicene and Post-Nicene Fathers of the Christian Church, Volume 10, St. Ambrose Select Works and Letters Second Series*. Grand Rapids, Michigan: Wm. B. Eerdmans Publishing Company, 1997.

Schaff, Philip D.D., LL.D. and Henry Wace, D.D., *A Select Library of Nicene and Post-Nicene Fathers of the Christian Church, Volume 11, Sulpitius Severus, Vincent of Lerins, John Cassian Second Series*. Grand Rapids, Michigan: Wm. B. Eerdmans Publishing Company, 1994.

Schaff, Philip D.D., LL.D. and Henry Wace, D.D., *A Select Library of Nicene and Post-Nicene Fathers of the Christian Church, Volume 13, Part II Gregory the Great, Ephraim Syrus, Aphrahat*. Grand Rapids, Michigan: Wm. B. Eerdmans Publishing Company, 1997.

BIO

The Rev. Jeffrey P. Johnson is superintendent of the Mid-America Conference of the Free Methodist Church of North America (FMCNA). He has served the Lord for 22 years as a pastor and missionary. As executive director for Men's Ministries International, he travels around the world teaching on evangelism and discipleship. He serves Butterfield Memorial Foundation, World Methodist Council Executive Committee, Wesley Commission, FMCNA Board of Administration and Central Christian College of Kansas. His wife, Yasmin Johnson, is a professor of nursing at Oklahoma Baptist University; they have two children, Ian Wesley and Isabella Anna Pauline.

Jeff has traveled throughout Asia as well as living in China for three years. He conducts Schools of Discipleship for churches interested in making disciples and promoting community renewal. He has ministered in more than 60 countries and oversees works in Guatemala and the Middle East.

Jeff earned a B.A. in history and an M.A. in education from Oral Roberts University and a doctorate in spiritual formation from George Fox Evangelical Seminary. He is an oblate in the Order of St. Benedict connected to St. Gregory's Abbey and University in Shawnee, Oklahoma.

Erin Smith is the administrator to the Mid-America Conference and the Midwest City Free Methodist Church. She is also the worship leader for the church. She served as chair for the Deaconess Pregnancy and Adoption Services; as chair for Mid-America Conference Women's Ministries International; and is the conference secretary of the Mid-America Conference. Erin earned a Bachelor of Musical Arts from Oklahoma Baptist University.

Her husband, the Rev. Jeremy Smith (Free Methodist elder) is a hospice chaplain; and they have two children, Caleb and Jacob.

CPSIA information can be obtained at www.ICGtesting.com
Printed in the USA
LVOW12s0132190615

442913LV00001B/1/P